D1062305

Architects of the Information Society

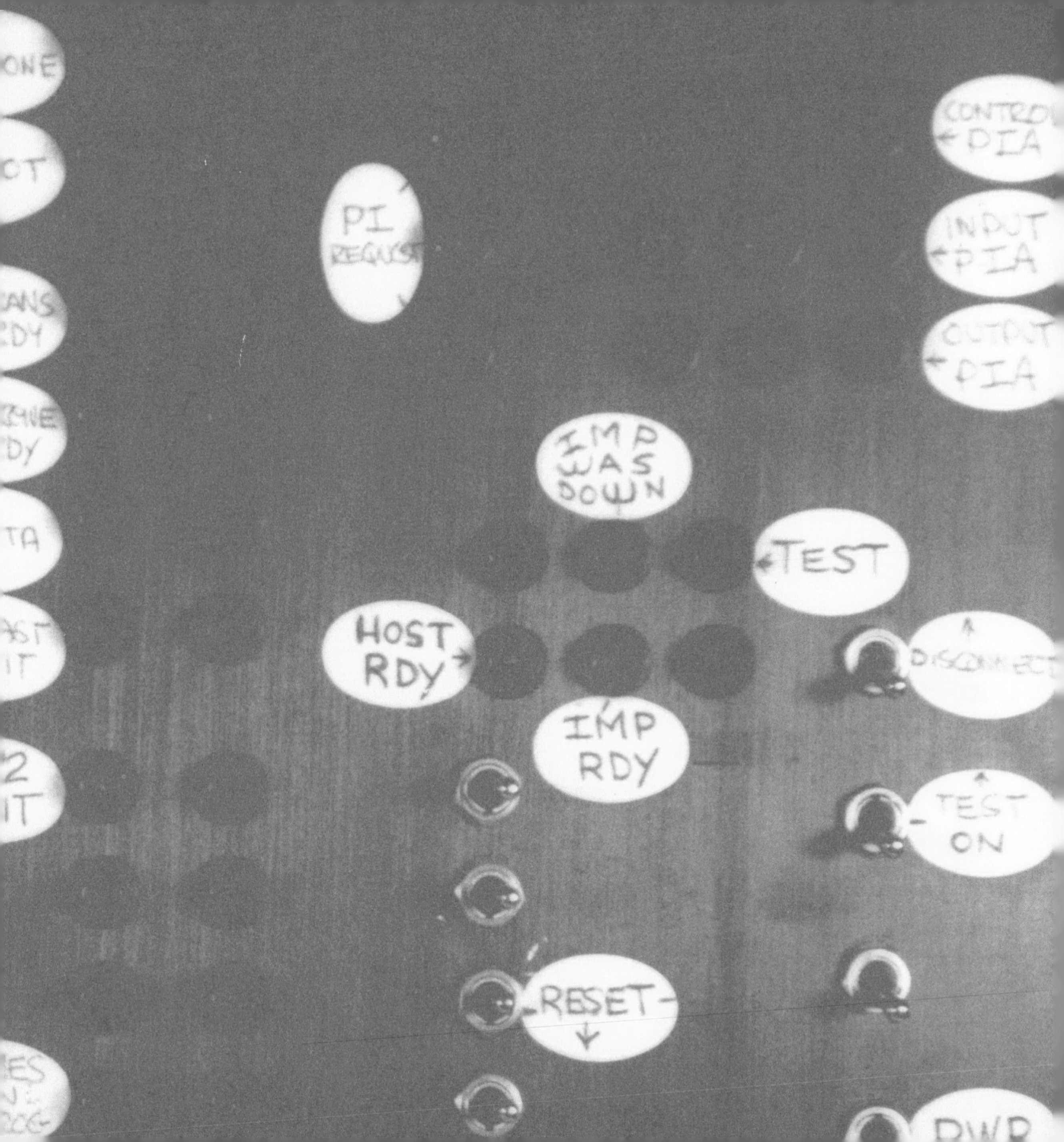

ONE

CT

ANS
RDY

ONE
RDY

TA

AST
IT

2
IT

ES
N
CG

PI
REQUEST

IMP
WAS
DOWN

HOST
RDY →

IMP
RDY

RESET
↓

CONTROL
← PIA

INPUT
← PIA

OUTPUT
← PIA

← TEST

↑
DISCONNECT

↑
TEST
ON

PWR

Architects of the Information Society

Thirty-Five Years of the Laboratory for Computer Science at MIT

Simson L. Garfinkel

edited by Hal Abelson

The MIT Press
Cambridge, Massachusetts
London, England

© 1999 Massachusetts Institute of Technology

All rights reserved. No part of this book may be reproduced in any form by any electronic or mechanical means (including photocopying, recording, or information storage and retrieval) without permission in writing from the publisher.

This book was set in Filosophia and Rotis San Serif by the MIT Press and was printed and bound in the United States of America.

Library of Congress Cataloging-in-Publication Data

Garfinkel, Simson L.
  Architects of the information society: 35 years of the Laboratory for Computer Science at MIT / Simson L. Garfinkel; edited by Hal Abelson.
      p.   cm.
  Includes bibliographical references and index.
  ISBN 0-262-07196-7 (hc: alk.paper)
  1. Massachusetts Institute of Technology. Laboratory for Computer Science—History.
I. Abelson, Harold. II. Title.
QA76.36.M37G36   1999
004'.0720744'6—dc21

                                                    98-43748
                                                        CIP

FLORIDA GULF COAST
UNIVERSITY LIBRARY

Contents

Preface   vii

1   The Computer Utility   1

2   The Intergalactic Network   21

3   The Information Marketplace   41

The Next Thirty-Five Years   65

Name Index   71

Preface

There is a short movie about student life that used to be shown by the Lecture Series Committee at the Massachusetts Institute of Technology. The short, which was filmed sometime in the 1960s, features a nerdy student in a suit sitting at a large machine, slowly punching a program into a deck of cards. The movie cuts away and shows other scenes from around campus, but it keeps coming back to the nerd, as his deck of cards grow taller and taller. Towards the end of the movie the nerd picks up his stack, which is now nearly two feet tall, and carries it to the MIT Computation Center. On his way there somebody bumps into him, and all of the cards scatter into a useless pile on the hallway floor.

Watching this movie from our vantage point at the end of the twentieth century, the tribulations of the nerd are comical. With our desktop computers, color screens, mice, voice recognition systems, and the Internet, it is nearly impossible to imagine just how far computation has come within the past four decades. The movie just cannot convey the frustration that computer users routinely felt back then. Computers of the time were slow, unreliable, and maddeningly difficult to use. They were also isolating, pitting the systems' management against the users and the users against each other. Looking back, it is easy to discount the heroic vision of the early computer pioneers, to look at the developments of the past forty years and think that each invention logically followed from the previous one. And, indeed, many people think that this is the case. At a computer conference in California, I once heard a speaker describe how companies had created local-area networks (LANs) in their offices, then created the Internet by tying those networks together. Little did the speaker realize that it was the ARPAnet, the precursor to the Internet, that paved the way for the original LANs. And then there was the time, at a coffee shop in Cambridge, when I heard two businessmen praising Microsoft founder Bill Gates for having the vision to invent Windows and bring it to the marketplace. Little did they realize that nearly all of the "breakthrough" technologies in Windows had actually been invented more than thirty years before, just a few miles from where they were sitting. Books about the history of computer science are becoming increasingly popular. We can attribute the popularity, in no small part, to the impact that computers have in our daily lives and the obvious importance that they will have in the next millennium. Unfortunately, like the businessmen in the coffee shop, the vast majority of these books have emphasized the contribution that companies have made to history, minimizing or overlooking entirely the contribution of academic research laboratories. Doing so is a great disservice—to the researchers as well as to readers and, indeed, to history.

The corporate vision of computers in the 1960s was a vision of large, expensive machines that provided essential record-keeping for large corporations and governments. Neither the users nor the manufacturers of those systems would have considered using them for education, interpersonal communications, or entertainment. And, just as important, the computers of the day were evolving in a different direction. Computers were not getting smaller: they were getting bigger, faster, and increasingly complicated. It is in that alien past that MIT's Project MAC was conceived and born. From the very beginning, Project MAC set out to change the computational landscape to support interactive processing. It was a formidable task, one with many different avenues that needed to be pursued. The scope of the project was evident in its very name: MAC was an acronym with not one but two meanings. Computers of the time were huge and expensive. The first job of the scientists at MIT was to perfect a way for many people to use a computer at the same time, so that they could break away from the dreaded world of batch processing and interact directly with the computer. Thus, the initials "MAC" stood for "multiple-access computer." And what would these people be doing with the computer? Some of them would be system programmers, no doubt, both using and extending the underlying operating system. But others would have the mission of finding new uses for the machine—education, medical diagnostics, writing, and even entertainment. For these people, the initials "MAC" meant "machine-aided cognition."

Project MAC got its start in 1963 with a two million dollar grant to MIT from the Department of Defense Advanced Research Projects Agency. Housed in MIT's Technology Square, in Building NE43, the Project immediately became a renowned research center at the forefront of computer science. Although it was initially thought to be a temporary endeavor, as the years passed it became increasingly clear that computing would be a fertile area of research for years to follow. In 1970, roughly a quarter of the researchers split off to form the MIT Artificial Intelligence Laboratory. Then, in 1975, the Project MAC itself was renamed the MIT Laboratory for Computer Science.

About This Book

This book is not the history of Project MAC or the MIT Laboratory for Computer Science, nor even a survey of their most significant contributions— many important research projects are not even mentioned here. Instead of writing a history, we have decided to explore three major, tightly interwoven themes that have been fundamental to the work at Project MAC and LCS.

The first essay takes a look at the primary task that Project MAC set out to do, the building of a "multiple-access computer." Although practically every computer sold today comes with an operating system that can run more than one program at a time, the computers of the 1950s and 1960s could not. To make a computer usable for more than one person, or even for more than one program, the researchers at Project MAC had to perfect a technique known as time-sharing, literally the sharing of a computer's attention between more than one task.

In the second essay we look in detail at the growth of computer networks, an unknown idea at the time when Project MAC was first conceived. One of the great unanticipated discoveries of Project MAC was that when more than one person can use a computer at the same time, those people will use the computer to communicate with each other. A few years later, ARPA commenced funding research on computer networks to allow people on different computer systems to communicate as well. Once again Project MAC was at the forefront of computer research, with one of the first ARPAnet connections. In the years that followed, researchers and alumni from Project MAC were instrumental in the creation of the Internet, local area networks, and systems for providing network security against attackers.

The third essay explores how networked computer systems have influenced and will continue to influence our economy and society. We examine the vision of the Information Marketplace—an economy based on the exchange of information, rather than on transportation of physical objects.

Acknowledgments

As a journalist, I have long been interested in the history of computer science. As an MIT alumnus, I have long been impressed by the critical role that the Institute has played in advancing the field. Over the years I have written many articles about MIT's contributions, but most of the articles focused on the advances of the 1980s and '90s; the early years of Project MAC and the formation of the MIT Laboratory for Computer Science had always been fuzzy and confusing for me.

Then last summer, Professor Hal Abelson asked me if I would be interested in writing a short book celebrating the thirty-five years of MIT's Laboratory for Computer Science. I had known Professor Abelson since I took the course Structure and Interpretation of Computer Programs with him and Professor Gerry Sussman in the fall of 1984. Since then I have had the privilege of working with him on many projects. Nevertheless, I was somewhat apprehensive about this project. It seemed so big, and the deadline seemed too tight. How could I do the research, tell a compelling story, and put the whole thing together in time for the LCS celebration in April '99?

The answer, of course, was that I could not do it alone and, fortunately, had help. Besides suggesting the book, Hal Abelson agreed to be my editor. Hal worked with me to decide which stories we would tell and which we would have to forgo. He suggested people at the Lab for interviewing and was able to supply many facts that I would have otherwise missed as a result of my age or lack of experience. Hal mercifully cut words when necessary, and added his own when appropriate. As with any good editor, it is only with great effort that I can tell where my work leaves off and where Hal's starts. This book is as much his as mine.

A large number of professors, researchers, and LCS staff took time from their busy days to speak with me about their work and the history of the laboratory. Likewise, a significant number of individuals who are not affiliated with the Lab but nevertheless intertwined with its history also saw it fit to answer my e-mail messages and telephone calls. Although I hesitate to list them all here, for fear that I may inadvertently miss one or two, both propriety and heartfelt gratitude demand that I specifically thank Tim Berners-Lee, David Bridgham, Vint Cerf, Dave Clark, Fernando J. Corbató,

Michael Dertouzos, Bob Fano, Bob Frankston, Bernard S. Greenberg, Richard Greenblatt, Gail Jennes, Frans Kaashoek, Tom Knight, Robert Metcalfe, Marvin Minsky, Peter G. Neumann, Tom Pinckney, David Reed, Ron Rivest, Jerry Saltzer, Jeff Schiller, Richard Stallman, Peter Szolovits, Tom Van Vleck, Patrick H. Winston, and Victor Zue.

Some of this book was based on interviews that I have conducted over the past two decades, first as an MIT undergraduate and then as a journalist. For those interviews, I can additionally thank Whitfield Diffie, Jim Gettys, David Gifford, Paul Gray, Steve Lerman, Joel Moses, Clifford Neuman, Adi Shamir, and David Wilson.

In the LCS office, Julie Kavanaugh Peisel supplied us with a wonderful list of LCS spin-off companies. Peter Elias provided us with useful information from the LCS 25 celebration. Rebecca Bisbee at the Artificial Intelligence Laboratory and Michael Yeates at the MIT Museum helped us look for photographs to illustrate this book.

At MIT Press Robert Prior proved invaluable for his vision and skill at negotiating, which made this book possible. Deborah Cantor-Adams did a wonderful job as our production editor, and Yasuyo Iguchi created a beautiful design. Terry Ehling, Terry Lamoureux, and many other people at MIT Press have contributed to the quality of this book and to completing its publication on a very tight schedule.

Finally, I would like to express my thanks to my agent, Lew Grimes, and to my wife, Beth Rosenberg, both of whom supported me to all ends in this project.

Architects of the Information Society

The Computer Utility

If computers of the kind I have advocated become the computers of the future, then computing may someday be organized as a public utility just as the telephone system is a public utility. . . . The computer utility could become the basis of a new and important industry.
—John McCarthy, speaking at the MIT Centennial in 1961

The information society was born in the spring of 1963 with the founding of MIT's Project MAC. Computers, of course, had already been on the scene for a quarter century, and information processing had already revolutionized the practice of science, engineering, and commerce. But the step from information processing *systems* to information *societies* was first achieved at MIT in Project MAC. This evolution was nurtured and refined by MAC and its descendants, the MIT Artificial Intelligence Laboratory and the MIT Laboratory for Computer Science.

Information societies are bonded through a shared computing and information infrastructure, and they could not exist without the technologies that make this sharing possible. The critical sharing technology that sparked the formation of Project MAC was time-shared computing.

The first computers, built in the 1930s and 1940s, were single-user machines—if only because so few people knew how to use them. But by 1955 most computers built for business, government, and universities were not

personal, hands-on machines at all. They were so expensive to buy and operate that the only way people could justify their cost was to keep the machines computing around the clock, using 100 percent of the available time. Thus was born the concept of batch processing.

"Batching was part of the efficiency game," says Fernando J. Corbató, who was associate director of MIT's Computation Center at the time. "You would prerecord all of the jobs on tape and then run them tape to tape." The programs would run through the computer like a train of boxcars through a granary, with the computer reading one tape, executing its commands, and writing the results onto a second tape.

Batch processing made programming a hard task. To create a program, you would write out on paper each line that the computer was supposed to execute. The program would be punched onto cards, usually by a keypunch operator, and the cards would be submitted to the computer facility's staff. The cards were recorded on a tape, the tape would run, and the results of the output tape would be sent to a line printer. Sometime later you would get the results of your job back.

"As people got more and more efficiency minded, they tried to milk the machine for more and more cycles," says Corbató. "The user got squeezed out more and more. Universities suffered the most because they did not have a lot of excess computer power. The queues for getting a job processed got to be from twelve to twenty-four hours."

Batch processing was a long, drawn-out affair. It was also a solitary affair. When a program ran, it ran alone on the bare machine. Other than by punching a second deck of cards, there was no easy way for the computer's users to share information. Indeed, batch processing created a kind of anticamaraderie: if many people were lined up to use the machine, it would take longer before you would obtain your results.

But there was a way to turn the tables on the machine. Corbató and others called this technique *time-sharing*.[1] Instead of devoting its computing

The Project MAC computer room on the ninth floor of MIT's Tech Square (facing page)

powers to one task at a time, a time-sharing system would work on many tasks simultaneously. Instead of forcing users to punch their programs onto cards and bring them to a central computing facility, a time-sharing system would be connected to dozens of computer terminals scattered around campus—in research groups, in computer clusters, even in professors' offices. The computer could switch among the different jobs so fast that each user would have the illusion of real-time, interactive use of the machine.

Interactive time-sharing was first conceived by John McCarthy, who began working on it in 1957 when he came to MIT on a Sloan Foundation fellowship from Dartmouth College. By 1959 McCarthy and his colleagues, including Steve Russel and Arnold Siegel, had permission to modify MIT's IBM 704 to create a rudimentary interrupt mechanism, and they were able to demonstrate a single-terminal online Lisp system at a meeting of the MIT Industrial Affiliates. By 1960 IBM had been persuaded to modify the Computation Center's 7090 for time-sharing, and an ambitious NSF-funded project to produce a three-terminal system was underway under the direction of Herb Teager, who took over the time-sharing project, since McCarthy wanted to focus on artificial intelligence.

McCarthy had also explained his ideas to Ed Fredkin and J. C. R. Licklider at the Cambridge consulting firm Bolt Beranek and Newman. They decided that time-sharing would be feasible on Digital Equipment Corporation's first computer, the DEC PDP-1, and Fredkin designed an interrupt system to allow this. Soon afterward, when DEC donated a PDP-1 to the MIT Electrical Engineering Department, Jack Dennis and his students began work on their own PDP-1 time-sharing system. [2]

As work at the MIT Computation Center continued, some researchers worried that Teager's plans were too ambitious. Corbató recalls how he " and a couple of key programmers"—Marjorie Daggett and Bob Daley—began work on the side on an "interim" project called the Compatible Time-

Sharing System (CTSS), using some of the NSF funds that had been allocated for the main time-sharing research. In November 1961, a crude prototype system with four terminals was running on an IBM 709, and the system switched to the Computation Center's IBM 7090 in the spring of 1962.

By *compatible* the engineers meant that the computer could run the time-sharing experiments while still providing batch operations. Indeed, aside from the fact that the batch jobs ran a little more slowly, the computer's paying users could not tell that the computer was running other jobs at the same time.

"If the auditors had come in they might have jumped on me for having misused the machine," Corbató chuckled some thirty years later. Instead, the rogue operating system became the first building block in the history of Project MAC.

The second building block fell into place in the fall of 1962 when Licklider was recruited away from BBN to a two-year stint at the U.S.

Fernando J. Corbató (left) and Jerome H. Saltzer standing before a block diagram of the Multics system, circa 1973

Department of Defense's Advanced Research Projects Agency (ARPA), where he become the founding director of ARPA's Information Processing Techniques Office (IPTO). Licklider, an experimental psychologist who had encountered the Whirlwind and TX2 computers at Lincoln Laboratories, was excited by the potential that interactive computing held—and he was determined to help realize that future. So instead of waiting for grant proposals or putting out a request, Licklider spent his first year on the job traveling to the country's major research facilities, trying to coax them into action. One of his first stops was MIT.

J. C. R. Licklider

"It was pretty clear that he wanted some big project at MIT," says Bob Fano, who was a professor in MIT's Electrical Engineering Department at the time and perhaps the one faculty member in a position to make such a project happen. Fano had learned to program in the late 1950s by working on a problem in coding theory for a faculty course in which the "computer types" in the Electrical Engineering Department, including Corbató and McCarthy, taught the others to program. But Fano understood that the computer had a far greater potential as a general-purpose simulation system. Anything that could be described step by step could be realized. "Because of this animal called a *computer*, any operation that was logically possible could be implemented. Anything was possible," he says, reliving his excitement and awe. Other MIT faculty members had been attracted to the idea of time-sharing, including McCarthy and Marvin Minsky. But Fano had come to the conclusion that the study of computing was ripe to emerge as an academic discipline, and that MIT should start a research laboratory for computation.

Over Thanksgiving week 1962, Fano attended a conference held for the Air Force in Virginia. Licklider was also there, and on the train home on Wednesday the two discussed the possibility of a large, ARPA-funded project at MIT. Licklider told Fano that ARPA could grant MIT more than two million dollars in 1963, and three million the following year, if Fano could just come up with a way to spend it all.

"It was a lot of money," Fano remembers. Fano spent Thanksgiving Day pacing around the house, and finally resolved to go ahead. The Tuesday after Thanksgiving, he met with MIT President Jay Stratton, who encouraged him. A proposal was on Licklider's desk two months later.

At first, the project was called simply *FF*—short for *Fano's Folly*. Soon the word *Project* was added; Fano knew that he would be starting a new research lab, but he wanted to call it a project so that he could grab people from other MIT laboratories without making them resign their positions.

Finally, the initials *MAC* were adopted at a dinner party on the night of April 1. Minsky, McCarthy, and Fano were all there. After hours of discussion, Fano decided on the name MAC, an acronym with two meanings: *machine-aided cognition* as the goal and *multiple-access computer* as the tool.

•   •   •

The nascent Project MAC focused on a new, ARPA-funded IBM 7094 mainframe computer, the CTSS operating system that ran on it, and a vision of

Bob Fano

computers as the intellectual power plants of the future. "Our goal was a computer utility," says Fano. "We wanted the user to regard the system as something that was there and reliable."

Key to this reliability was a computer program (designed by Corbató himself) for backing up the IBM mainframe's five megaword disk file to tape. The backup had to be reliable because the disks were not. "Corby had thought through the operation of that system beautifully," recalls Fano. "He is a public utility engineer. . . . He had the backup all organized. In the beginning there were two hours a day devoted to copying the whole file to tape. . . . And then he developed the continuous backup, so that it was copying in the background. . . . It was a very, very important thing to gain the trust of the community—to stop people from punching cards." Information kept on punch cards would not be available for sharing.

Project MAC was created to explore a shared computing resource. But unwittingly, a second experiment was unfolding: the sharing of an online storage system, a way for people to share each other's data and programs, was creating not just a public utility but an *information community*. As Fano and Corbató wrote in *Scientific American* in 1966,

> The system makes it possible for the users to carry on a discourse with one another through the machine, drawing on its large store of knowledge and its computing speed as they do so. The time-sharing computer system can unite a group of investigators in a cooperative search for a solution to a common problem, or it can serve as a community pool of knowledge and skill on which anyone can draw according to his needs. Projecting the concept on a large scale, one can conceive of such a facility as an extraordinarily powerful library serving an entire community—in short, an intellectual public utility.[3]

Early on, Fano and the rest of MAC's management realized that writing a computer program and making it available for public use was a lot like writing an article for an academic journal: it took the knowledge that one researcher had discovered and made it generally available. As more and more users wrote programs that were generally usable, Project MAC created an editorial review board to decide which programs would become part of the system library, where they could be easily accessed by all of the computer's users. Commands were being added so quickly that the decision was made to put their documentation online so that any user could print the instructions as needed. The TYPSET program for inputting the documentation and the RUNOFF program for formatting the printout—designed by graduate student Jerry Saltzer as a diversion from working on his thesis—together became the world's first word processor.[4] Another set of commands was created so that the systems users could send electronic notes to tell each other about new developments. This became one of the world's first e-mail systems.

One day in 1964 Fano arrived at his office to find Joseph Weizenbaum waiting for him, glowering.

"What's the matter?" Fano asked.

"The MAC system was not working last night," growled Weizenbaum. "I was told it would be working this morning. It's not working now. What the hell is going on?"

Weizenbaum's outrage, recalls Fano, was "the expression of the customer of a public utility." Fano turned to Dick Mills, his assistant director, and smiled. "We've done it!" he said.

●　　　●　　　●

Even though some users were treating the computer as a public utility, the CTSS system had a long way to go before it a could match the reliability of real public utilities. "A public utility must be available to the community twenty-four hours a day and seven days a week without interruption," wrote Fano and Corbató.[5] But CTSS could not provide nonstop operation because it had to be shut down for repairs, modifications, and additions to the system. These failings were not unique to CTSS: they were shared by every computer system that had ever been built.

Corbató knew how to build a reliable system. The secret was redundancy:

Every part of the system should consist of a pool of functionally identical units (memories, processors, and so on) that can operate independently and can be used interchangeably or simultaneously at all times. In such a system any unit could be taken out of service for repair or maintenance during a period when the system load was low, and the supervisor would distribute the load among the remaining units.[6]

Two years before publication of the *Scientific American* article, Project MAC had already embarked on a program to build such a system, to be called *Multics,* short for *MULTIplexed Information and Computing Service.* Reaching beyond MIT, the project also involved the Computer Department of the General Electric Company, which was building the computer's hardware, and Bell Telephone Laboratories in New Jersey, which decided to collaborate with MIT with the expectation that Multics would become the next central computing facility for the Labs.

The principal motivation behind CTSS was simply to demonstrate that time-sharing was feasible. As a result, a lot of corners were cut. With Multics, the Project MAC team decided to do everything right from the beginning. For example, one of the happy discoveries of CTSS was that time-sharing made it possible for computer users to build on each other's work. But CTSS did not make this sharing easy. Multics, on the other hand, was designed to share data, programs, and other computer resources in an efficient yet highly secure fashion. If two users wanted to run the same program at the same time, Multics would load only a single copy of the program. Virtual memory, combining for the first time ideas from the Manchester University Atlas and the Burroughs computers, would prohibit different user programs from trampling on each other's memory. Memory rings of protection—a concept invented by Bob Graham and Ted Glaser and implemented in hardware by Mike Schroeder—enabled different programs running on behalf of the same user to have different levels of access to the machine's operating system and hardware.

Multics was an astoundingly ambitious operating system—perhaps a little too ambitious. Originally the project was supposed to take just two and a half years. By early 1969, with no end in sight, Bell Labs withdrew. But the Multics ideas were infectious. Two of the Bell researchers who had worked on the project, Ken Thompson and Dennis Ritchie, decided to continue developing some of the ideas —most notably the Multics tree-structured file system—on their own. By cutting corners, they had a prototype working by the end of the summer. Peter Neumann, another Bell researcher, suggested that Thompson and Ritchie call the operating system *UNICS*, a pun that meant *castrated Multics*. Eventually, the Bell crew changed the name of their operating system to *UNIX*.

Meanwhile, work on Multics progressed at MIT. Two months after UNICS, the first Multics became operational in October 1969 for general campus use, and responsibility for its operation was transferred from Project MAC to the MIT Information Processing Center. A year later a second site was set up, at Griffiss Air Force Base in Rome, New York, where the system was used for processing data from classified intelligence studies. By the end of 1971, the MIT Multics installation was operational twenty-four hours a day, seven days a week, and served a community of more than 500 users. Project MAC had truly created a computer utility.

Multics fulfilled virtually all of Corbató's goals. For example, the system at MIT had two central processing units and three memory banks. During peak times these could all run as a single machine. At other times, the system could be partitioned into two smaller systems—one for operational use and a separate development system for use by staff. The world's first hot-swap system for processors and memory, designed and implemented by Roger Schell, allowed Multics to be reconfigured without rebooting. Few computer systems built since have enjoyed such flexibility.

Alas, the developmental system came too late to prevent MAC's largest schism—a fight between those who saw the project's central computer system primarily as a utility to support research and those who saw it as a subject of research itself. "Management felt that it had to be reliable and keep working. The AI people wanted a machine they could tinker with. Tinkering and reliability were different objectives, and it was difficult to maintain those on the same computer," says Saltzer, who was a graduate student at Project MAC before becoming a professor there in 1966.

Joel Moses, sitting between a
high-speed line printer and an
interactive teletype, circa 1964
(facing page)

Unofficially, Project MAC was rechristened "Minsky against Corby," after the two individuals who personified the battle. Under Minsky, the AI team got its own computers—a series of PDP-6, PDP-7, and PDP-10 computers from the fledgling Digital Equipment Corporation. Team members wrote their own operating system called the *Incompatible Time-Sharing System (ITS)*—a direct slap at Corbató. In 1970, Minsky seceded from Project MAC altogether and created the MIT Artificial Intelligence Laboratory.

.   .   .

After the completion of Multics and the departure of the AI researchers, a kind of postpartum depression settled in on Project MAC. For the first seven years of its life, MAC's central mission was the development of time-sharing. Now things were shifting from a single, focused project in operating systems to a broader family of discipline-oriented research efforts. In 1968, Licklider replaced Fano as director and started a major thrust in human-computer interfaces and interactive modeling. In 1971, Ed Fredkin took over and started several new initiatives, including work in automated medical diagnosis. Michael Dertouzos became the fourth director of Project MAC in 1974. One of his first actions as director, in 1975, was to change the name of the project to LCS, the MIT Laboratory for Computer Science.

"Project MAC sounded like a hamburger," remembers Dertouzos, who picked the new name with Joel Moses, the lab's associate director.

"The Lab drifted," says Saltzer. "By the 1970s [the Lab] had expanded to the point where [CTSS and Multics] were only a piece of the action—by 1975, a small piece." The tightly knit community, which had been formed and held together by the magic of time-sharing, fragmented. And with the emergence of relatively low-cost minicomputers, individual groups within the lab were able to purchase their own computing equipment.

Meanwhile, the attention of some researchers at LCS was changing from operating systems to hardware. What was making this possible was a new generation of integrated circuits called *microprocessors*—single chips that contained almost an entire computer. The first microprocessor was created to run a desktop calculator. The second microprocessor operated a video terminal.

Many scientists at MIT and elsewhere regarded these new microprocessors as toys. But a few researchers realized that they were the future. One of those researchers was Steve Ward—another faculty member who had come up through the ranks as a Project MAC graduate student.

"By the late 1970s I was interested in using these exciting microprocessors to build systems," says Ward. "At that point, there was a real dichotomy between the world of minicomputers and bigger things, and the world of microprocessors. I decided, with some students who subsequently became faculty members, that . . . we would build a New Machine. We would base this [New Machine] on microprocessors and run a real OS on it, and the whole future would be these things on people's desks."

Rather than picking a particular microprocessor for his *NuMachine,* as it was eventually called, Ward designed a computer architecture that would work with any microprocessor. At the heart of this system was a computer bus for moving information between system units—a bus he called the *NuBus.* Compared to the other complicated buses at the time, the NuBus was unique in that "it was stark in its simplicity," he says.

The NuMachine needed an operating system as well. Multics was out of the question: the time-sharing operating system was too big and too complicated and required special-purpose hardware that was conceptually elegant but had never been adopted by the mainstream computer industry. Ward's group started to write its own operating system called *Trix.* "It was a network-oriented OS and had a lot of features that are just now becoming popular in operating systems." But group members soon realized that building an operating system was not where their interests lay, and Trix "never got beyond a research project."

Fortunately for Ward, by 1980 the community of computer researchers had grown from a few labs to a few dozen—and for the most part, the research community was moving in one particular direction: UNIX, the castrated Multics operating system that had been spawned from Bell Labs. UNIX was loved because it was small and portable, which meant that it would be easy for Ward to get the operating system running on the NuMachine. The group got the UNIX source code from Bell Labs and ported the operating system to three different microprocessors: the Zilog Z8000, the Intel 8086, and the Motorola 68000. Although it would not be clear for several years, by building a single-user computer with a bitmapped display, a network interface, and a powerful microprocessor, Ward's group had just created one of the world's first UNIX workstations.

Over the next decade, Ward's group became a clearinghouse of sorts for UNIX operating system ports. Many companies that created commercial UNIX workstations, including Sun Microsystems, started with a UNIX system that had either been sent to them from LCS or was directly descended from another system that was. Ward's group also left its impact on the world of microcomputer design: when Apple realized that it needed a bus for its Macintosh II computer in 1985, it chose Ward's NuBus—which was by then nearly a decade old but still on the leading edge. The computer community was expanding from academia to the marketplace. Over twenty years, the number of people benefiting from technology developed by Project MAC and LCS had grown from a few dozen researchers around MIT to millions of computer users around the globe.

•   •   •

Computers have changed dramatically over the past thirty-five years, but the fundamental design of operating systems has remained more or less constant. Like CTSS, today's operating systems consist of application programs, which respond to the needs of the user, and a supervisor program, which manages the underlying hardware "kernel-level" resources such as input and output devices. When the user runs a program, the supervisor loads the program into memory and gives it temporary control of the machine. When a user program needs to access kernel-level resources, such as during input and output, requests are handled through special services provided by the operating system.

A fundamentally new approach to operating systems is now under development at LCS. Called the *Exokernel*, the system puts application programs directly in control of the kernel resources: the only service provided by the supervisor is a basic level of protection. This can result in impressive performance gains, without compromising reliability or security of the underlying computer system. The Exokernel charts a new direction for operating system evolution. "An Exokernel eliminates the notion that an operating system should provide abstractions on which applications are built. Instead, it concentrates solely on securely multiplexing the raw hardware," explains Frans Kaashoek, who is overseeing the research.

The Exokernel is ideal for applications that demand high performance, such as Web servers or laboratory control systems. In performance testing, the LCS group's Cheetah Web server, a server that is specially designed to take advantage of the Exokernel, can run eight to ten times faster than a conventional Web server in a UNIX operating system running on the same hardware. And because of its compact size and closeness to the hardware, the Exokernel is well suited to mobile computing applications.

Not surprisingly, the Exokernel's user community is starting out small: today there are probably fewer than a hundred people who are experimenting with the Exokernel, says Kaashoek. But unlike the early days of CTSS and Multics, the Exokernel is being created by a loose collaboration of computer users all over the world. This research and thousands of other scientific projects are direct descendants of the intellectual public utilities engendered by Project MAC.

Yet the vision of MAC's founders encompassed more than just collaborative community research. In the 1966 words of Fano and Corbató,

> Looking into the future, we can foresee that computer utilities are likely to play an increasingly large part in human affairs. Communities will design systems to perform various functions— intellectual, economic, and social—and the systems in turn undoubtedly will have profound effects in shaping the patterns of human life. The coupling between such a utility and the community it serves is so strong that the community is actually a part of the system itself. Together the computer systems and the human users will create new services, new institutions, a new environment, and new problems. . . . To what ends will the system be devoted, and what safeguards can be designed to prevent its misuse? It is easy to see that the progress of this new technology will raise many social questions as well as technical ones.[7]

Thirty-five years later, we can read these words as prophetic of the global information infrastructure and the World Wide Web, the promise they hold for society, as well as the challenges they pose. But the transition from information communities to an information society requires a technological jump beyond the operating systems that enable people to share a single computer. For this, we must turn to a second critical technology pioneered in MIT computer research—computer networks.

Notes

1. The original MIT time-sharing demonstrations were called *time stealing*, since they allowed "important" professors in the MIT Computation Center to run their jobs without waiting for long batch-processing jobs to finish.

2. Credit for the idea of time-sharing is also widely attributed to the British computer pioneer Christopher Strachey, who described it in a talk at a UNESCO conference in 1959 (C. Strachey, "Time Sharing in Large, Fast Computers," *Proceedings of the International Conference on Information Processing*, UNESCO, London: Butterworth's, June 1959, 336–341). Strachey described the critical architectural extensions, such as priority interrupts and memory protection, required for time sharing. His vision of time-sharing was that several operators would be able to use the machine at the same time to run mostly batch jobs, with perhaps one simultaneous debugging session, rather than the interactive system being developed at MIT. For more on the early development of time-sharing at MIT and on the relation between Strachey's and McCarthy's visions, see McCarthy's 1983 note "Reminiscences on the History of Time Sharing," available at http://www-formal.stanford.edu/jmc/history/timesharing/timesharing.html.

3. R. M. Fano and F. J. Corbató, "Time-Sharing on Computers," *Scientific American*, 215, no. 3 (September 1966): 128–140.

4. The thesis that Saltzer was avoiding, completed in 1966, concerned the Multics processor multiplexing system. This was probably the world's first threads package and first description for what is today known as *symmetric multiprocessing*.

5. Fano and Corbató, "Time-Sharing," 129.

6. Ibid., 134.

7. Ibid., 140.

The Intergalactic Network
2

It is not proper to think of networks as connecting computers. Rather, they connect people using computers to mediate. The great success of the internet is not technical, but in human impact.
—Dave Clark[1]

Batch processing did not generate much need for computer networks. But as soon as CTSS was up and running on a regular basis, the value of a network became self-evident: people all over MIT's campus wanted to log in.

Fortunately for the members of Project MAC, the idea of remote access was not without precedent. As far back as the 1930s, the Bell Telephone Laboratories had been exploring techniques for sending data over telephone lines for early fax and telephotography machines, and several devices were produced for the air defense system in the 1950s. In 1962 AT&T introduced the Bell 103 *modem* (short for *modulator/demodulator*), which could transmit and receive data at the blinding speed of 300 bits per second—nearly three times as fast as a teletype could print! By 1965 MAC's IBM 7094 was perhaps the world's most connected computer, with more than two dozen modems that could be dialed from anywhere on the MIT campus—or anywhere in the world. It also had interconnections with the TELEX and TWX networks, so that any teletype could connect to the MAC system.

Project MAC time-sharing system. Photos from *Scientific American*, 215, no. 3 (September 1966): 128 (on facing page)

But there was a problem: time-sharing was playing havoc with the Institute's telephone service—a massive relay system located next to the Building 10-250 lecture hall. "The pattern of the interconnections among the relays was designed by telephone engineers in the 1930s with all of the standard assumptions—that only 10 percent of the phones would be in use [at a time] and that you would have three-minute calls," explains Jerry Saltzer.

Time-sharing put very different demands on the phone system: a typical call lasted from thirty minutes to several hours, and almost all the computer's lines were in use during business hours. As a result, people calling in would get busy signals even though CTSS had free ports available. "You would pick up the phone and get blocked because there were not enough paths through the switch," says Saltzer.

The solution was to build a second switch for data communications. Saltzer and a few others dug out AT&T manuals from the 1930s and discovered which assumptions made in designing a system for voice were inappropriate for data. Then they started buying equipment in configurations that the phone company could not understand. Ultimately, most members of Project MAC ended up with two telephones on their desks: one connected to MIT's voice switch and a second one for the terminal connected to the data switch—the world's first computer network.

•   •   •

Shortly after Saltzer joined the faculty in 1966, a new graduate student named David Clark arrived at Project MAC. Clark had cut his programming teeth writing a punch-card-based operating system for an IBM 1620 while he was an undergraduate at Swarthmore College. A master at assembler programming, Clark soon found himself working for Saltzer on the Multics "gate keeper"—the part of the operating system that managed the interface between user-level programs and the secure Multics operating system kernel.

Despite his experience in system programming, Clark's academic research concerned computer languages and formal definitions. Then in 1969 disaster struck: Clark's advisor suddenly left the MIT faculty and moved to California. Clark turned to Saltzer for help.

Saltzer could not support Clark's work on languages, but he did have open projects pertaining to the certification of Multics as a multilevel secure operating system. Saltzer's dream was to have Multics certified as provably secure, but as things stood, the system's kernel was far too complicated to make any definitive claims. "Jerry had a whole list of subsystems he thought we could throw out of the kernel," recalls Clark. "And he said to me, 'I want to see if you can throw all of the I/O architecture out of the kernel because it has nothing to do with security.'"

Clark spent the next four years enmeshed in the intricacies of the Multics General Input/Output Controller, but his finished thesis was not entirely successful:

> I wrote down all of the strategies for doing I/O outside of kernel space. . . . But the one thing I realized I could not move out of the kernel . . . was the network because the network was a shared device at the logical level. You didn't know whom a packet belonged to until the packet was in memory and you could look at the header. And that required running code. So at the end of my thesis, when I turned it in, I said, "Well, I moved everything out of the kernel except the network. But you know? The network is really weird. It's really different. It's not an I/O device. It's a whole new class of thing." And Jerry said, "Well, yeah, I don't know what to make of that, although you are obviously right."

Jerome H. Saltzer (right) and Michael D. Schroeder, circa 1973

The "network" that Clark was wrestling with was the ARPAnet, the world's first packet-switched computer network. Like MAC's time-sharing, the ARPAnet was the godchild of J. C. R. Licklider. A psychologist by training, Licklider was fascinated by the potential of computers to enhance human communication. He playfully christened the cadre of computer experts he assembled at the IPTO "the Intergalactic Computer Network" in a self-mocking exaggeration of the community spirit he'd seen grow up around the first time-sharing system. Yet his vision of computer communication was in earnest. Together with Bob Taylor, who succeeded him as head of the IPTO in 1966, Licklider prophesied, "In a few years men will be able to communicate more effectively through a machine than face to face."[2]

Inspired by Licklider's ideas, Taylor convinced the U.S. Department of Defense to fund the creation of a national network to link research computers around the country. To head the project, Taylor chose Larry Roberts, an MIT computer scientist from Lincoln Laboratories. Taylor unveiled plans to construct a network of Interface Message Processors (IMPs) at an ARPA Principal Investigators' meeting in 1967. In August 1969 the first IMP was delivered to UCLA, which would serve as the Network Measurement Center for the incipient "ARPA Network."

By 1971 MIT had its own IMP, and engineers throughout Tech Square were busy interfacing it to Project MAC's computers. The Multics interface was a large wire-wrapped circuit board called *Fred the ABSI (Asynchronous Bit Serial Interface)*, which is still in Clark's office. It was built by Rick

Gumpertz, with Clark writing the software. The PDP-10 code, meanwhile, was written by Bob Bressler and used a hardware interface built by an MIT graduate named Bob Metcalfe.

•   •   •

Metcalfe was something of a curiosity at Project MAC. Graduating from MIT in 1969 with dual bachelor's degrees in electrical engineering and management, Metcalfe had gone "up the river" to Harvard for graduate school, where he had been granted a fellowship in Division of Engineering and Applied Mathematics—what passed for Computer Science at the nation's oldest university.

"As a graduate student I naturally fell into working on the ARPAnet and quickly learned to hate Harvard," recalls Metcalfe. Harvard, explains Metcalfe, had treated him to an elaborate game of bait and switch, awarding him a full scholarship for his first year as a graduate student and then yanking it. "Apparently that was standard operating procedure, but it really pissed me off," he says. A friend of Metcalfe's introduced him to MAC Research Scientist Al Vezza, who hired Metcalfe to build the IMP interface for the PDP-10.

"As more machines joined the ARPAnet, implementers found that not every machine could communicate with every other one. So in October 1971 MAC sponsored an ARPAnet system programmer's workshop. "We built a big matrix and tested interoperability among the sites," Metcalfe remembers. "This would be perhaps the first meeting of the IETF [Internet Engineering Task Force]. We would find bugs and fix them, then try again, find another bug and fix it—all while we sat there. It was really cool. . . . Lots of sites got connected, and the matrix was filled in substantially."

To conduct the actual survey, Metcalfe wrote a program called *ping* that would open a connection across the network to see if the other side was responding. It was the first time that the word *ping* was used in conjunction with computer networking.

"The big lesson there was that interoperability hadn't been tested," says Metcalfe, looking back. "Theoretical compliance with the standard does not work."

As soon as Multics and the other machines were hooked up to the IMP, a curious fact was discovered. Even though the intended purpose of hooking to the ARPAnet was to let the computers at MIT communicate with machines at other research sites, almost all the ARPAnet traffic that originated at the MIT computers was going to other MIT computers.

"From our point of view, [the ARPAnet] was the local-area network for the building," remembers Saltzer. "The fact that there were also connections to San Francisco was interesting, but the main purpose was to move files from the AI machine the DM [Dynamic Modeling] machine."

There was so much intra-MIT traffic, in fact, that BBN decided to specifically subtract it from the official ARPAnet statistical accounting. "Such traffic was called 'incestuous,' and it was subtracted from the total because it was an embarrassment," explains Metcalfe. "We were trying to build a network that would connect the world, not MIT." In the process of avoiding embarrassment, BBN fumbled the opportunity to invent local-area networking.

Metcalfe wrote his Ph.D. thesis, a long dissertation on the current state of packet network technology, and accepted a job at Xerox's Palo Alto Research Center starting in the summer of 1972. But just as he was leaving for Silicon Valley, the unthinkable happened: he failed his thesis defense. The committee complained that his work was not sufficiently original. PARC representatives told him to come anyway because they needed him to build an ARPAnet interface for one of their computers.

Bob Metcalfe as an undergraduate at MIT

Shortly after moving to California, Metcalfe took a trip to Washington, D.C., and stayed at the house of Steve Crocker, an ARPA program manager. Crocker had just finished meeting with Norm Abramson, who had built a packet radio network called *Aloha Net* to connect computer installations on the Hawaiian Islands. "I was enchanted with the chutzpah of simply having all the terminals send whenever they needed to and sorting out the collisions after the fact," Crocker recollects. "If I recall correctly, there was a proceedings from a major computer conference with a description of Aloha. I put it on my coffee table at home and pointed it out to Bob as I unfolded my sofa bed for him that evening."

Metcalfe read the proceedings and realized that packet transmission and collision detection could be incorporated into a small-scale network suitable for connecting together machines within a single building or even within a single room. Instead of sending data by radio, the signal could be transmitted on a piece of coaxial cable. Metcalfe called the system *Ethernet.*

Xerox included Ethernet in its Alto personal computer. Metcalfe, meanwhile, rewrote his thesis, this time with an emphasis on Aloha and a theoretical foundation for the new Ethernet technology. Harvard accepted the thesis for graduation, but it was published by MIT as *Project MAC Technical Report #114.* "A Harvard Ph.D. thesis published by MIT—that gives you the bottom line," snorts Metcalfe. "I didn't like Harvard; Harvard didn't like me."

• • •

By the mid-1970s, the ARPAnet had spawned other packet-switched networks. But the networks were disjointed: each one could share information only among its own nodes. What was needed was a mechanism to allow all these networks to communicate—to form a single, overarching internetwork, or *Internet.* The solution was developed by Vint Cerf at UCLA. A stream of information would be split into packets according to a new standard called the *Transmission Control Protocol* (TCP). The TCP header would serve as an envelope that masked the (possibly incompatible) internal data structures used by the different networks. Gateway computers on each network would process the header information and forward the packets to the destination hosts, which would remove the headers and process the data.

Back at the newly renamed MIT Laboratory for Computer Science, Clark had hooked up with graduate student David Reed. "He looked at the early spec of TCP, and he said, 'This is really complicated, this is much too complicated,'" remembers Clark.

Reed invented his own technique called the *Data Stream Protocol* and showed it to ARPA. According to Clark, Cerf wrote back that he was not looking for competition to TCP, but if Clark and Reed would like to participate in the design work for TCP, they were more than welcome. Thanks to their involvement, TCP was split into two protocols: TCP, which handled data encapsulation, and IP *(Internet Protocol)*, which handled routing. The two together became known as TCP/IP. "I like to think that I'm responsible for the slash," says Reed, who joined the LCS faculty but soon drifted from the world of protocol design. "Reed got bored," Clark recalls. "But I thought it was fascinating, so I got sucked in."

Two groups at MIT embarked on developing local-area network technology. At the AI Lab, a group of researchers led by Tom Knight and Jack Holloway decided to clone and improve Ethernet. They called the new system *ChaosNet*. The AI Lab's network ran over cable-TV cables, which MIT had recently pulled throughout campus in preparation for the Institute's MIT-TV Project. From its inception in the mid-1970s until it was replaced in the mid-1980s, ChaosNet was MIT's primary campus network backbone.

Meanwhile, at LCS Clark's group was creating a fundamentally different network technology. Instead of coaxial cable, the network relied on two pairs of twisted wires. Today you can walk into any computer store and buy $35 interface cards that send data at 100 megabits per second over a twisted-pair cable. But in the 1970s, says Clark, people did not think merely that such speeds would be difficult: "They literally thought it was impossible. It's remarkable what happens when you say, 'It's impossible, but I'm going to do it anyway.' . . . We bought large spools of twisted pair, and we said, 'You know, you can send bits a lot faster down this stuff than people think. Why are people so resistant to twisted pair?' We decided that we could build a 10 megabit version."

Today's office local-area networks are descended both from Ethernet and the twisted-pair network. They still use the same Ethernet protocols that Metcalfe helped invent. But the physical layer uses Clark's twisted pair.

As time went on, Clark became increasingly involved with the low-level protocols of the Internet itself. At first, Saltzer was skeptical that specializing in protocols was a good idea. "Are you sure that protocols are a really significant topic of intellectual study? They're just documents about headers. They just explain headers," he said.

In the years following, Clark and his group proved just how worthy a pursuit protocols actually were. In July 1982 he published the "David Clark Five"—five Internet standards documents that detailed how to make the network protocols run properly and run faster, for example, by assembling packets without excessive copy operations or by batching characters to avoid sending a packet for each character. This also included the first set of suggestions and guidance on designing routers.

First ARPAnet hardware interface at Project MAC, placed in service in 1972 between a Digital Equipment Corporation PDP-10 model KA (known as

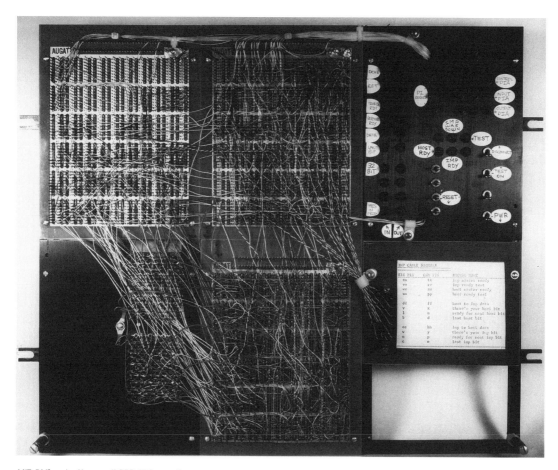

MIT-DM) and a Honeywell DDP-516 operating as an
ARPANET Interface Message Processor. Removed from
service in 1984. Constructed by Bob Metcalfe.

"We teach students to write a program. They know they have to debug it until it is correct," Clark cautions. "We don't teach students to debug for performance." In 1981, Cerf appointed Clark to be chief protocol architect for the Internet—a position he held until 1989.

.   .   .

While Clark worked to make the Internet run faster, his former boss Jerry Saltzer worked to see how large a network could be built using the TCP/IP architecture. His laboratory was the entire MIT campus, testbed for a $70 million experiment called *Project Athena*.

Project Athena grew out of a 1979 report of a committee, cochaired by LCS Director Michael Dertouzos and MIT Director of Information Systems Wes Burner, that was chartered to develop a plan to address MIT's computing needs over the coming seven years. The idea of using computers for education had been one of the principal motivations for time-sharing back in the 1960s: Corbató had written that time-sharing would be the only way to make computer resources plentiful enough on campus that machines could be used to help teach courses. Multics had occasionally been used for classroom work in limited ways. But the committee report noted the relatively small role of educational computing at MIT and recommended the establishment of a campuswide network with five mainframe computers connected to about 400 terminals, "for instructional and medium-size research computing."[3]

The 1979 recommendation was largely ignored by the MIT administration. "There was relatively little interest in some schools and none in others," recalled Dean of Engineering Gerald Wilson in a 1988 interview. But in the School of Engineering, the idea took hold and grew. "[EECS Department Head] Joel Moses had a vision that every student should have a personal computer and they should be linked in a local net," remembers Saltzer. "Gerry Wilson wanted to see computers enhance education at MIT."

In 1982 Wilson and Moses decided that the School of Engineering should proceed on its own. They decided to partner with Digital Equipment Corp. and build a School of Engineering computer facility. After Michael Dertouzos negotiated to get 2000 workstations from DEC, MIT President Paul Gray "thought that we really should do this for all of MIT," says Wilson. "We were asked to go back and see if we could get additional resources."

At roughly the same time, officials from IBM contacted Jerry Saltzer. IBM had

Michael Dertouzos

heard rumors of a big project between DEC and the School of Engineering and wanted to be involved. Saltzer arranged a meeting that included several IBM executives and Dertouzos and Moses, and a deal was struck in short order. Digital and IBM would provide $50 million in hardware, maintenance, and expertise; Digital's computers would go to the School of Engineering, while IBM's equipment would go to the rest of the Institute. MIT would provide faculty, students, technical staff, and $20 million in development support.

The ambitious goal of Project Athena was to create a new generation of software that would revolutionize undergraduate education. In the process, the Institute would build the world's largest system of networked *workstations*, a new generation of computers based on high-speed micro-processors and bitmapped graphics. With Digital and IBM both in the mix,

Athena called for a system that would be "coherent"—where students could sit down in front of any Athena computers on campus, irrespective of the computer's manufacturer, and share applications and software. As Dertouzos and Moses wrote in an early plan for Athena,

> In small communities of 20 to 50 people who use a single time-shared computer, coherence already exists at the operating system level, since there is a single operating system common to all users. Coherence above this level, i.e., in the domain of application programs, has not been widely demonstrated over a community as large as the School of Engineering. . . . Coherence across a distributed system with several hundred, let alone a few thousand, computers has not yet been demonstrated.[4]

Athena set up shop in 1983. At its head was Civil Engineering Professor Steve Lerman—an appointment that underscored Athena's mission as one of creating educational software, not innovating fundamental computer science technology. The project planned to use off-the-shelf hardware and system software from IBM and Digital. What Athena's early management team did not realize was that the two computer giants could not deliver on their promises of a unified and coherent networked campus computer infrastructure—largely because the technology to create such a system did not exist.

Athena purchased fifty VAX computers from Digital and set them up around campus as time-sharing machines, each running a copy of Berkeley UNIX and supporting four dumb terminals. After that the project stalled. Finally, in the fall of 1984, Wilson asked Saltzer to step in as Athena's technical director. "I didn't replace Lerman," says Saltzer. "He took the flack, and I worked on the technical side. That actually worked pretty well."

Fred the ABSI (Asynchronous Bit
Serial Interface) was the interface
between the MIT Multics computer
and the ARPAnet IMP (Interface
Message Processor)

One of Athena's most serious technical challenges was the
"coherence" mandate: How could
one design uniform software for
the Digital and IBM machines
when the graphical application
programming interfaces they pre-
sented were so different? Luckily
for Saltzer, a solution was already
underway by the time he arrived at
Athena, pioneered by Jim Gettys,
a Digital engineer assigned to
Athena, and Bob Scheifler, an LCS
researcher working for Barbara

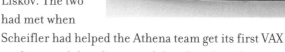

Liskov. The two
had met when
Scheifler had helped the Athena team get its first VAX
working, and they discovered that they shared a common
problem—how to take advantage of the UNIX workstations.

"An overeager Digital salesperson had sold
Barbara's group half a dozen VS100s [bitmap displays
that plugged into a Unibus on a VAX]. We [at Athena]
were expecting an order of 100 of them," recalls Gettys.
"The only software for the VS100 for UNIX at the time . . .
was a basic device driver and a port of a simple window
system called W done for the Stanford V system by Paul
Asente and Brian Reid. It presumed fast RPC [remote
procedure call], which UNIX systems weren't all that
great at, so it didn't perform very well." Scheifler and
Gettys decided to cooperate to build an improved version

of W as a joint LCS/Athena effort. Gettys explains, "We couldn't call it *W* anymore (since it wasn't) but acknowledged the ancestry by calling it *X*."

According to Saltzer, "My contribution on [X] was limited to recognizing that Gettys's argument was correct—that a window system was an essential component for Athena's success—and not killing [the project]." But Saltzer made another important contribution by convincing MIT to distribute X under "a copyright that I had worked out together with Larry Allen in the systems research group at LCS. Similar in goal to [Richard] Stallman's approach, the copyright gives blanket permission to anyone to distribute, modify, and sell the software as long as MIT is credited. That copyright allowed Gettys to convince virtually every engineering workstation vendor in the world to adopt X windows."

MIT began distributing X in 1984, and by 1986 X had become the de facto graphics interface for UNIX workstations. In 1988 LCS established the MIT X Consortium, with Scheifler as head, to promote continued development and dissemination of the window system. Five years later the Consortium was spun out of MIT as an independent concern, and in 1997 it transferred responsibility for X to the Open Group. In 1998 X is still vital and growing, through its incorporation into free GNU/Linux implementations for personal computers.

A second technical challenge to Athena was security, a long-time concern of Saltzer's stemming from his efforts to secure the Multics kernel—techniques that had previously been classified by the U.S. military but had increasing commercial significance as well. "In the early 1970s I realized that key distribution was important for network security and worked with some people inside the classified arena to get the basic idea declassified." As the ideas became public starting around 1974, Saltzer began including material on key distribution in his undergraduate operating systems course, 6.033. In 1978, Mike Schroeder, a former LCS professor working at PARC, and Roger Needham, a researcher from the Computer Laboratory at

Cambridge University, published a seminal paper presenting a new key distribution protocol, which launched serious public discussion of the challenges in network security.[5]

In 1984, Clifford Neuman, an MIT undergraduate completing a thesis under Clark's supervision, developed an implementation of the Needham–Schroeder protocol extended to provide centralized management of authorization policies. Neuman subsequently joined Project Athena, where Saltzer suggested that, together with Steve Miller, he redesign the protocol to improve its suitability for integration with applications, so that it could be used to secure Athena's network services. The result was the Kerberos authentication system, which, following Needham and Schroeder, was distinguished by that fact that passwords travel over the network only in encrypted form.

To Athena's developers, it seemed obvious that a large network would be subject to attack by "sniffers," so that it would be mandatory to encrypt network traffic—especially sensitive data like passwords and keys. In this, Athena was well ahead of its time. "I was really shocked that it was nine more years before sniffers became recognized as a problem," says MIT Network Manager Jeff Schiller, one of the initial contributors to the Kerberos design and today IETF area director for security. Today, with security an acute concern in electronic commerce, Kerberos and Kerberos-derived authentication systems are becoming critical components of any network infrastructure.

Project Athena produced some outstanding educational software, particularly in aeronautics and modern languages, although it never really delivered on its promise of large-scale educational change. Athena's planners underestimated the difficulty and expense, both in dollars and faculty time, required for sustained curricular innovations. On the other hand, the technical achievements that came under Saltzer's direction—the realization of Licklider's "Intergalactic Network" vision on a universitywide scale—set the tone for networked computing throughout the world. Ironically, starting in 1996 the computer industry's new hot marketing idea has been "the networked PC," a personal client machine running server-based software with the help of a window system and secured by a network authorization. How many of the earnest marketers promoting this "new computing paradigm" realize that such a system has been running at MIT for the past fifteen years?

Notes

1. Quoted in G. Malkin, "Who's Who in the Internet?" Internet Engineering Task Force, Request for Comments No. 1336, May 1992.

2. J. C. R Licklider and Robert Taylor, "The Computer as a Communication Device," in *In Memoriam: J. C. R. Licklider 1915–1990*, Digital Research Center, Palo Alto, California, August 7, 1990, 21; originally published in *Science and Technology* (April 1968).

3. Report of the Ad Hoc Committee on Future Computational Needs and Resources, Massachusetts Institute of Technology, April 1979.

4. Michael Dertouzos and Joel Moses, "Educational Computing," MIT School of Engineering, January 5, 1983 (memo).

5. R. M. Needham and M. D. Schroeder, "Using Encryption for Authentication in Large Networks of Computers," *Communications of the ACM*, 21, no. 12 (December 1978), 993–999.

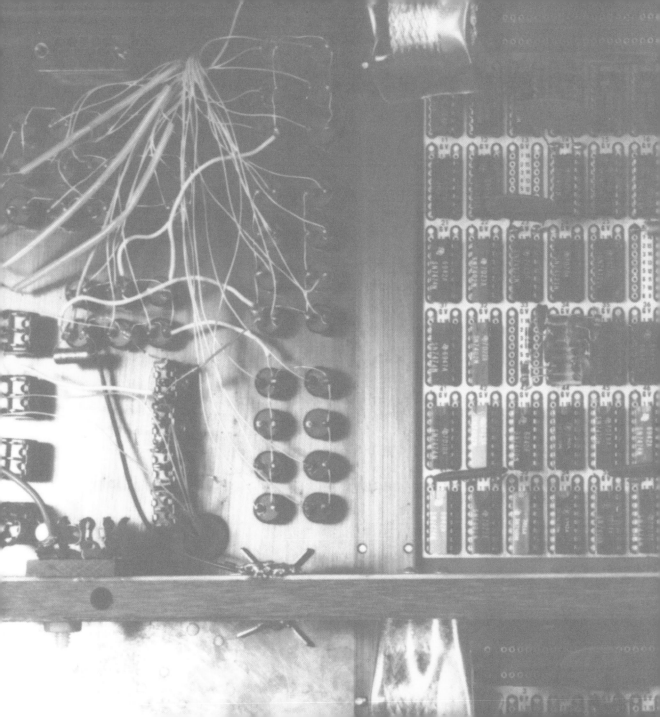

The Information Marketplace 3

By Information Marketplace *I mean the collection of people, computers, communications, software and services that will be engaged in intra-organizational and intra-personal information transactions of the future. . . . The Information Marketplace already exists in embryonic form. I expect it to grow at a rapid rate and to affect us as importantly as have the products and processes of the industrial revolution.*
—Michael Dertouzos, 1980 [1]

The way that people interact with their computers has changed little since Project MAC's inception in 1964. The operator sits at a desk and types on a keyboard; the computer responds by displaying messages on a screen or sending text to a printer. Even so-called revolutionary advances like mice and graphical user interfaces have done little to change this fundamental paradigm. Computing is still an activity that's best done at a desk. And while people frequently use computers to communicate with others, the actual human-computer interaction is something that's best done alone. Another thing that has not changed much in thirty-five years is the way that people use computers to work with information. Computers have enabled people to handle more information, but they have done it by giving us tools for working *faster* and not necessarily *smarter*. The Internet has brought tremendous information resources to our fingertips, but it has done a lousy job of reducing the data into valuable knowledge. The current generation of computers has turned us into incredibly efficient, incredibly fast file clerks, but it has not relieved us from the burden of managing our own files. Instead, we are drowning in data.

•   •   •

As LCS moves into its next thirty-five years, the way we use computers and access information is about to change fundamentally—largely because the current trends are not sustainable. As ever-expanding computer networks bring more data within our grasp, our computers will necessarily have to do a better job of preprocessing this sea of information for human consumption. As computers become smaller and more portable, and as they become increasingly ubiquitous, we'll be communicating with computers without resorting to keyboards and screens.

Victor Zue and the Spoken Language Systems Group at LCS are working on a system that has all these attributes. Called Jupiter, the program combines an automated Web browser, an intelligent database, a natural-language query and retrieval system, a voice-recognition engine, and speech synthesis. But none of this technology is apparent to Jupiter's users. They simply call a toll-free number and ask Jupiter about the weather.

"Hi, welcome to Jupiter, the MIT Lab for Computer Science weather information system," says the computerized voice that answers the phone. "This call is being recorded for product development. How can I help you?"

"What is the weather in Cambridge tomorrow?"

There is a brief round of music—it sounds like the theme from a quiz show—and then the computer starts talking again. "I know of a Cambridge, England, and a Cambridge Massachusetts. In Cambridge in England Monday: cloudy, high 44. Low 34. What else would you like to know?"

Victor Zue, senior research scientist and associate director of LCS

"How about Cambridge, Massachusetts?" the caller asks.

"In Cambridge in Massachusetts this afternoon: sunny, high 45 to 50. Tonight 30, partly cloudy. What else?"

"That's all," says the human. "Thank you very much."

"Thanks for using Jupiter. Have a nice day!"

Victor Zue beams like Giapetto, proud at seeing his handicraft successfully mimicking a human being. Like a human, Jupiter is tolerant of small mistakes that people might make in asking their questions. Jupiter understands the different ways that the same question could be phrased. And Jupiter can handle the inherent ambiguity in human conversation. Rather than give error messages, Jupiter tries to give answers. When it does not have enough information, it either sounds apologetic or tries to cover its weaknesses. "What we are trying to do is [to take] a more human-centric point of view," Zue explains. "Rather than make humans do things the way machines can handle them, what we are trying to do is make machines accommodate what humans are doing."

Fundamentally, Zue is trying to invent a new kind of interface between computers and humans, one that's based on conversation instead of typing. "It is a modality that is intended not to replace other modalities but to augment them so that the user would have a choice," he explains.

As Jupiter shows, there is more to building a new interface than combining a speech recognizer with a speech synthesis device: for people to converse with computers, the two need to have something to talk about.

That's the other side of Jupiter: the system continually scans the Internet for new weather reports, downloads them into a client/server database, and handles queries phrased in English rather than in computerese. Complicating the task are annoying technical details, such as Web sites that present data in different formats and unreliable sites that offer data on some days and withhold it on others. Jupiter hides these problems from users, letting them concentrate on the weather rather than the data.

Success has brought its own problems, of course. "At first when our system came out, people said, 'It sucks because it doesn't understand what I am saying.'" Zue recalls. Since then the system has improved immeasurably. "Today," he says, "They say, 'It sucks because it sounds like a robot.' Originally we didn't have speech synthesis on our radar. We started working on synthesis by demand."

     •   •   •

This goal of having computers gather information, reduce it, and present it in a manner palatable for humans has been part of LCS since the conception of the information utility. Licklider, as MAC's second director, started a new research group in 1968—the Dynamic Modeling Group—one of whose goals was to simplify human-computer interaction through visual interfaces. But the absence of inexpensive display technology made the project too far ahead of its time, and the group eventually refocused its efforts on programming technology.

By the mid-1970s, though, systems such as the memory-mapped displays invented by Tom Knight for the AI Lab in 1972 had begun to appear at a few research laboratories, and people at LCS and elsewhere realized that easy-to-use computers would eventually be a part of everyday life. Michael Dertouzos had been director of LCS for less than two years when a reporter from *People* magazine walked into his office to interview him about "the role of computers in our lives."[2]

The interview was prescient in many ways. At the time, the popular image of computers was one of huge, expensive, formidable devices. The reporter was captivated by the vision of intelligent machines portrayed in films like *Colossus: The Forbin Project*—omniscient juggernauts that could subjugate humanity and take over the planet. But the researchers at LCS were already living in a different world, a world of networked computers and distributed systems. It was a world in which information, not hardware, was ascendant. And it was a world, Dertouzos was convinced, that the rest of humanity would soon be joining.

"In ten or fifteen years, [a computer] should cost about the same as a big color TV," Dertouzos told the interviewer. "This machine could become a playmate, testing your wits at chess or checkers. If a computer were hooked up to API or UPI newswires, it could be programmed to know that I'm interested in Greece, computers, and music. Whenever it caught news items about these subjects, it would print them out on my console—so I would see only the things that I wanted to see," he said in 1976, describing a popular research project of the day.

The reporter wanted to know if computers could "run a war" or wage one against humans. Unlikely, said Dertouzos. It was far more probable that they would be delivering our mail. "Will the computer eventually be as common as the typewriter?" she asked. "Perhaps even more so," the director answered. "Don't be surprised if there is one in every telephone, taking over most of the dialing."

Dertouzos kept thinking about this vision of the future after the reporter left—the idea of a computer in every home. "I was convinced that there would be one computer in every three homes within a decade," he remembers.

J. C. R. Licklider (on right) and two members of the Project MAC Dynamic Modeling Group

But what would people do with these new machines? They would do the same thing that people were doing already, Dertouzos realized, except that the computers would let people do these things faster and more efficiently.

"I could see very easily that all these machines would be networked. That was no stretch. . . . And that's where I conceived of the notion of the *Agora*—the flea market."

It was an image from his childhood. When he was a young boy growing up in Athens, Dertouzos went shopping at the Agora every Sunday for tubes, power supplies, coils, and all kinds of electronic devices. "I was very much into electronics. I wanted to build transmitters," recalls Dertouzos, whose interest in radio was spawned by his father, an officer in the Greek navy. Using a set of high-power 6L6 tubes, he built a transmitter that could be heard throughout a quarter of the city.

The same sort of marketplace could be built in an information society, Dertouzos realized. "All these people would be around, they would be talking, they would do everything—buy, sell, exchange, gossip. It would be this great place where I used to go every Sunday. But instead of buying crystal radios, they would be buying and selling information and information services."

And there would be another important difference as well. In 1947, when Dertouzos was operating his radio transmitter, he did it all illegally. "I once had to dismantle everything in a hurry," he remembers, when Athenian police tried to track him down using sophisticated radio direction finders. But in the world of the Information Marketplace, people would be able to publish whatever they wished.

The idea of a world filled with computers was a familiar one in the science fiction of the day. But on Wall Street and in Washington, D.C., it would be years before the idea of an information-based economy would take hold. One of the major barriers to the future, a barrier that was being broken at LCS even as Dertouzos was musing about marketplaces, was the lack of adequate network security,

•   •   •

In fall 1976 Steve Boyack, one of Ron Rivest's graduate students at LCS, showed him a newly published paper by two researchers at Stanford

University. The paper described potential applications of a new kind of system for scrambling data called *public-key cryptography*.[3] With public-key cryptography, wrote Whitfield Diffie and Martin Hellman, people could exchange confidential messages without any prearranged "secret keys"—and still be assured that no one could intercept a message and learn its contents.

With public-key cryptography it would be possible for people to sign their names to e-mail messages and other digital documents in a way that if the document were ever changed—if even a single comma were replaced with a period—then the signature would no longer verify. There was just one problem with the paper: although Diffie and Hellman showed how to arrange for private communication (using a technique now called *Diffie–Hellman key negotiation*), their suggestions for implementing a full-fledged public-key system that would permit both confidentiality and signatures did not really seem workable.

Rivest was intrigued. He showed the paper to Adi Shamir and Len Adleman, who were also faculty members in the LCS Theory of Computation Group. The three talked about the problem at length and then decided to take up the challenge and develop a working two-key cryptographic system. Rivest, Shamir, and Adleman spent months trying to solve the riddle posed by Diffie and Hellman. Most of the time Rivest would propose new codes, only to have Shamir break them. At one point, they became so frustrated that they decided to try to prove mathematically that public-key algorithms were logically impossible.

Finally, in spring 1977, Rivest had a flash of insight. He was lying on a couch at home when he conceived of a method for performing encryption using modular arithmetic in such way that breaking the code would require factoring extremely large numbers, something that seemed computationally infeasible. When Shamir and Adleman heard the idea, they agreed that it worked.

Adi Shamir (left), Ron Rivest (center), and Len Adleman (right)

That summer, Martin Gardner, a columnist at *Scientific American*, learned about the technique and asked the three to devise a puzzle using the algorithm. They opened a dictionary at random, selected some words, used these to compose a secret message, and then scrambled the message in such a way that decrypting it would require factoring a 129-digit number. Factoring this huge number, Rivest told Gardner, was so difficult that it could not be solved for 40 quadrillion years. The encryption technique and the encrypted message were published in the August 1977 issue of the magazine. In the article, Gardner advertised that the LCS computer scientists (Rivest, Shamir, and Adleman) would send a copy of their paper describing the so-called RSA encryption algorithm to anyone who sent a "self-addressed, 9- by 12-inch clasp envelope with 35 cents in postage." More than 3,000 requests for the paper poured in. In December, after waiting for a determination by MIT's lawyers that sending out the paper would not violate U.S. law, Rivest, Shamir, and Adleman threw a pizza party at the Lab, where people stuffed envelopes for hours. The same month, the MIT Patent Office applied for a patent to the invention.

Waiting for MIT's lawyers was not mere overcaution. In September, the Information Theory Group of the Institute of Electronic and Electrical Engineers received a letter from the National Security Agency (NSA) containing a warning. According to the letter, the planners of an upcoming conference on cryptography that fall, which included Rivest, could be in violation of U.S. law. Foreign nationals might be in the audience, and cryptography was (and still is) subject to rigid export control regulations. The NSA later disavowed the letter, saying that the employee who had written the letter did so "on his own behalf."

The letter was just the beginning. Over the following years, LCS received pressure to ease off on cryptographic research. The NSA told Dertouzos and Rivest that the RSA algorithm had already been discovered by British Intelligence and that the technique was known to be flawed.[4] In 1980, Adleman (then on leave at the University of Southern California) was told that parts of his NSF proposal on cryptography research would not be funded by NSF for reasons of national security, and that funding would be provided by the NSA. He refused to agree to this funding arrangement, and NSF funded his work but included language in the grant letter making him responsible for seeking prior review on publication.

In attempts to clear the air, Dertouzos and Rivest held meetings in 1977 with government officials, including NSA Director Admiral Bobby Inman. The security establishment wanted the right to prior review of all LCS publications on cryptography: researchers would have to first clear their papers with the NSA before submitting them for publication. As Inman expressed in a public speech in 1979, "There is a very real and critical danger that unrestrained public discussion of cryptologic matters will seriously damage the ability of this government to conduct signals intelligence and the ability of this government to carry out its mission of protecting national security information from hostile exploitation."

LCS refused to agree to any prior-restraint conditions and offered a compromise. The researchers would include NSA on the list of close colleagues to whom they first normally sent their papers. If the government decided that something needed to be classified, it was welcome to initiate legal proceedings to attempt to prevent publication. But there would be no question of prior restraint and no question of MIT's need to seek permission before publishing. The NSA agreed to this and to this day has never sought to prevent publication of any LCS research.

MIT President Paul Gray subsequently met with Inman. "I made the expected arguments about academic freedom, the importance of free communication among workers in the field," recalls Gray of his meeting with Inman. "He was courteous, even charming, but didn't budge an inch."

In 1983 Rivest, Shamir, and Adleman founded RSA Data Security, with the goal of fostering practical applications of public-key encryption. "We put together a business plan thinking that secure telephones would be the place to start the business," remembers Rivest. While the company tried to finance and build a prototype, Rivest started working on a software implementation of the RSA crypto system that would demonstrate the technology. "The software was viewed as being for education purposes. One of the problems with encryption, particularly in those days, was that nobody understood it at all. So we were developing demonstration software to illustrate what public-key encryption could do," Rivest said.

After a few years of failing in the secure telephone market, RSA's management realized that making telephones secure "was not to be the best place to start the market." Meanwhile, the software demos turned into products, and the products created a market.

RSA's first big customer was Iris Associates, which built RSA's technology into a program called "Notes," which it was creating for the Lotus

Development Corporation. Its second licensee was Novell, which built the technology into Netware. It was then that the company realized that its best path to success was not by selling either hardware or software, but by selling "toolkits" that other companies could use to easily build the RSA algorithms into existing products.

It is hard to overstate the importance of the RSA algorithm in the information marketplace today. Public-key cryptography is the primary tool of the information age for protecting privacy and verifying identity. While other practical public-key systems have emerged since 1976, RSA is still the most widely used because of its flexibility, power, and security.

Rivest, Shamir, and Adleman are today all luminaries in the field of computer security. Rivest has remained at LCS, where he is now an associate director of the Lab and, together with Silvio Micali and Shafi Goldwasser, heads the Lab's Cryptography and Information Security research group, which continues to do world-leading work on both the mathematics and public-policy implications of cryptography. One area in particular where Rivest has been active is the determination of key sizes: if you pick a key that's too short, a message that you think is secure may be revealed in time.

No one knows the consequences of choosing a key that's too small better than Rivest himself. In April 1994, Rivest's home phone rang. It was Jeff Schiller, manager of MIT's networks, with a curious question: "Hey, Ron, what's a *squeamish ossifrage?*"

Rivest paused for a second and then began to laugh. Schiller, together with MIT undergraduate Derek Atkins, had coordinated a group of 600 volunteers around the world to factor the huge number and unscramble the secret message from the issue of *Scientific American* of seventeen

A printed circuit board from DEC PDP-6 serial no. 2 from the MIT AI Laboratory. Delivered October 6, 1964. Demolished February 16, 1982.

years before: *The magic words are squeamish ossifrage.* Rather than taking "
40 quadrillion years" (Rivest later admitted that he'd made up that number)
the codebreaking effort took about eight months. What had made the solution possible were the dramatic improvements in computer speed and in
factoring algorithms, combined with the Internet's ability to allow a large
group of people to collaborate on a shared computational problem.

•   •   •

By its very nature, an information marketplace needs information in
order to exist. But in the early 1980s, even after low-cost computers were
available, information was not. For the most part, information such as news
and business statistics was still being distributed in printed form rather
than electronic. And the computers of the 1980s were generally sold without modems or network connections. Although the technology for both
modems and network connections was well understood by 1983, companies
didn't sell these with new computers, since there were no readily available
services to use them with. Since few computers had modems or network
connections, few publishers saw the need to make their data available in
electronic form.

In the early 1980s LCS Professor David Gifford started experimenting
with a way solve this chicken-and-egg problem. Rather than building a new
network, Gifford decided to piggyback on the broadcast network, where
companies had already spent considerable effort to create a network that
could reach practically every home and business in the country.

Gifford developed a system for modulating computer data on top of
a standard FM radio station. Receiving the signal required a small box
that could be mass-produced at a cost of a few dollars. Called the Boston
Community Information System, the system broadcast news stories from

the *New York Times* and the Associated Press. Special software running on a home computer would scan the incoming articles and selectively "clip" those that the user wanted to see. The system was installed and run in Boston on a two-year test basis, from 1984 through 1986, and then continued afterward for participants who were willing to pay a nominal charge.

In order to restrict access to the information to those involved in the experiment, Gifford developed an encryption algorithm encrypting the data before it was sent. The algorithm was supposed to demonstrate to the news organizations that their content could be transmitted in the air and still protected. But the algorithm actually illustrated the difficulty of developing encryption algorithms and the importance of using algorithms that have been peer reviewed: ten years later, two cryptographers at University of Maryland, Thomas Cain and Alan Sherman—who had been a graduate student at LCS under Rivest—developed an effective attack against the algorithm, allowing them to discover an encryption key using only a single encrypted article. It took them only about four hours of computer time using a network of eight SPARCstations.

Gifford's Community Information System proved that there was a thirst for electronically distributed information. But the system was never profitable, largely because the scale was too small. Even a medium-sized metropolitan area like Boston does not have the sheer number of computer users to subsidize the fixed costs that are inherent in delivering information over a computer network. What Gifford needed was a larger user base—something national, or even global, in scale.

•   •   •

When Tim Berners-Lee first started talking about the Web in 1989, people in academic and research communities looked at it and shrugged. "The

Tim Berners-Lee

World Wide Web?" they asked, with a combination of amusement and scorn. "Isn't that being a bit pretentious?"

Perhaps so. For while Berners-Lee's Web was truly worldwide, it was not very substantial. Developed at CERN, the European high-energy physics center in Geneva, W3 was just another in a long series of hypertext systems to emanate from a research laboratory. Its main use was for publishing information on the Internet about physics and physicists, but fewer than a few dozen Websites existed on the entire Internet. Meanwhile, the Internet already had two other hypertext systems that were vastly more popular—one called WAIS, the other called Gopher. Why was Tim, as he insisted on being called, trying to create a third?

As the world was soon to discover, there was a fundamental difference between Berners-Lee's World Wide Web and the hypertext systems that had come before. Whereas earlier systems had been structured to access information on individual computers, the Web viewed the entire Internet as a uniform hypertext canvas, a space that people could navigate by clicking on simple links that could be embedded within any document. And while it was relatively slow to access information stored on another computer using previous systems, the Web introduced a fast new protocol called the hypertext transfer protocol (HTTP), also designed by Berners-Lee. For the first time, the Web made it possible to quickly view documents that were stored on another computer without first downloading the documents and storing them locally.

Besides inventing the underlying protocols, Tim oversaw the creation of a C language library of functions for transmitting information over the

Web, a Web server that ran on a variety of UNIX platforms, and an early Web browser that ran on workstations manufactured by NeXT Computers, Inc. By 1992 there were dozens of Web servers around the world, and the amount of Web traffic flowing over the Internet was steadily growing. Even at this early date it was clear that Tim was on to something big.

Unlike many who followed him, Tim chose not to commercialize his work so as to preserve the integrity of the Web as a universal medium. "If I had started WebSoft, Inc., that would have been the end of it," he says retrospectively. "The Internet community would have dropped the Web like hotcakes, just like a lot of people dropped Gopher when the University of Minnesota started charging."

But soon it proved equally clear that CERN would not be his home for long. The European physics consortium was interested in making fundamental discoveries in physics and not in building information infrastructures. Tim started thinking about finding a new home. In summer 1993, he ran into David Gifford on a bus at a conference in England. Gifford suggested that Web development move to LCS, and when he returned to Cambridge, he urged Dertouzos to make this happen. Before the end of the summer Dertouzos had flown to Europe to meet with Tim, and the two had laid the groundwork for the World Wide Web Consortium.

When Dertouzos suggested creating a consortium, he was speaking from experience. LCS was still basking in the glory of the X Consortium, which had taken the Project Athena window system and turned it into commercial products used by thousands of companies. Albert Vezza, the Lab's associate director who had been instrumental in forming the X Consortium and later spinning it out of LCS, was asked to take charge of organizing the new Web effort. To help on the European side, Dertouzos enlisted the aid of George Metakides, a long-time friend from Athens who was director of ESPRIT, the European Commission's information technologies program.

By spring 1994, the outlines of an organization were in place, to be based partly at LCS and partly at CERN with startup funds ensured both by DARPA and ESPRIT. In September, Tim joined LCS, and the World Wide Web Consortium (W3C) was officially launched from MIT with Vezza as chair and Tim as director. But in December, CERN decided to withdraw to begin a massive effort to construct the European supercollider that would require all their energy. With the European Commission's approval, the European center of the Consortium moved to INRIA.

W3C has since grown to include almost 300 member organizations and has established a third host center at Keio University in Japan. The Consortium defines the standards that ensure that different products created by different companies and inventors will be able to interoperate in the Web of the future. These include protocols such as HTTP for transmitting information, languages such as HTML in which Web pages are authored, and guidelines for creating multilingual Web pages and Web sites that are accessible to people with disabilities as devastating as blindness or as mundane as bad eyesight. The W3C is also increasingly active in the intersection between public policy and technology in issues such as privacy and shielding children from harmful material on the Internet.

In some ways, the Web has begun to realize the vision of the information marketplace. But it is really just the beginning. Today's Web is essentially an electronic publishing system; it lacks the elements of bargaining and negotiation that make a market function. Moreover, the structure of the Web—with its over-reliance on click-by-click browsing user

Albert Vezza, senior research scientist and associate director of LCS, 1990

interfaces—impedes automation. The Web uses computers to publish information to people—ignoring the power of providing that same information in a form that is easy for other computer programs to interpret. As Dertouzos writes, it is as if "the companies making the first steam and internal combustion engines of the Industrial Revolution made them so that they could work together only if people stood between them and continued to labor with their shovels and horse-drawn plows."[5]

Tim points to a similar problem. The Web protocols, he explains, deal almost exclusively with format rather than interpretation. You can use HTML to publish a calendar on a Web page that is formatted as a table so that browsers can display it correctly. But there's no standard way in HTML to indicate that a table is a *calendar* so that automated scheduling tools could traverse the Web and easily identify and process any calendars they encounter. Accordingly, one of the major thrusts of W3C is the development of formats for expressing *metadata*—machine-understandable information that can tag Web objects as calendars, bibliographic records, prices, contract terms, or all sorts of other things required for a functioning marketplace.

Metadata is more than a new set of HTML tags that say things like, "This is a CD title" or "This is a price." As envisioned by the W3C, metadata would be a comprehensive set of standards for describing data about data. For example, Web sites that sell shoes could create a standard set of HTTP queries for searching the company's database and a standard template for sending the data back. Other companies could then implement those same standards. Pretty soon, other groups could build a program that could scan the Web for the best bargains. "The long-term objective is the *automatable Web*—basically, to put machine-readable information on the Web," says Tim. "It could have a revolutionary effect."

Adding semantic tags to Web data will be an important step toward the information marketplace, but it is only a step. What is missing are systems that can negotiate a sea of data such as the Web but that can also model the real entities that data tags represent. It's systems like these that could finally address the promise of the information marketplace to truly improve human life through information processing. And nowhere does the promise of information technology to improve life seem so compelling as in automated medical care.

•   •   •

In 1971 when Ed Fredkin took over from J.C.R. Licklider as director of Project MAC, the organization was entirely funded by ARPA and tightly focused around operating systems. Fredkin made it a priority to extend the range of projects and to broaden the potential funding base. One promising was medicine, where Anthony Gorry, a student of Joseph Weizenbaum who had completed a Ph.D. in computer-aided medical diagnosis, was continuing this work as a faculty member. Fredkin decided that Gorry could be the catalyst for an expanded effort in medicine. In 1973 he staged a week-long brainstorming session at his resort in the Virgin Islands and invited Gorry and several MAC faculty together with physicians from the New England Medical Center (NEMC): Gerry Cuseur, Steve Pauker, and NEMC Director Bill Schwartz. One outcome was the formation of the Clinical Decision Making Group, with Gorry as head. Another was that over the following months, some of the MAC faculty, including Fredkin and Gerald Sussman, spent a day a week donning gowns and accompanying NEMC staff on their rounds in an attempt to learn something about medical diagnosis.

Peter Szolovits started working at the Clinical Decision Making Group in 1974. He had just joined the Lab as an assistant professor, intending to do research on knowledge representation systems with Bill Martin, who, together with Joel Moses, supervised the development of the Macsyma symbolic mathematical manipulation system.

"Bill was working at the time on automatic programming and knowledge-representation problems," recalls Szolovits. "I had done a Ph.D. on the construction of programs for specialists. We had built some English-like languages for an anthropologist who was keeping track of data on the 80,000 members of the Glemby Tonga Tribe in central sub-Sahara Africa." While developing those systems, Szolovits had become convinced that the largest barrier to making progress in the field of artificial intelligence was the difficulty of representing knowledge in a form that computers could understand.

Szolovits collaborated with Martin on knowledge-representation systems to model businesses and then got involved with some of Gorry's graduate students who were collaborating with NEMC doctors. When Gorry suddenly decided to leave MIT the next year and move to Rice University, the M.D.s decided to recruit Szolovits to fill Gorry's shoes. "So that's how I ended up running this group," he says somewhat modestly.

Simply stated, the goal of the LCS Clinical Decision Making Group is "to understand the intellectual processes of medicine and maybe to simulate them on a computer," says Szolovits. Over the past twenty years this group and others like it around the world have made substantial progress toward this goal. The group has developed a case-based reasoning system that can make medical diagnosis on cardiovascular diseases based on previous cases that it has encountered. A different approach to a similar program is taken by the Heart Disease Program (HDP), which asks questions about a patient and formulates a diagnosis. And the group is now working on a new computer program, called GENINFER, that will assist genetic counselors in evaluating the risk of recurrence of genetic disorders based on the analysis of family pedigrees.

Programs like HDP and GENINFER will occupy a special place in the information marketplace: by combining book knowledge with algorithmic modeling, they'll be in a position to help humans predict their own personal future. By folding the statistical tabulation of vast medical databanks and analyzing outcomes of people in similar situations, the descendents of today's programs will be able to give medical consumers realistic appreciations of the options that they face.

Unfortunately, that future is still a long way away. "If the truth be told, almost none of this stuff has been really used in a clinical setting," says Szolovits. The reason, he says, is that the data that these programs need to run reliably simply are not available in the typical clinical information system. "Typically all one can do is test these systems in an experimental situation where you are willing to hire clerks to type in the data." The problem, quite simply, is that a tremendous amount of information recorded at hospitals is still recorded on paper—if it gets recorded at all.

This is one impetus for the group's Guardian Angel project, a collaboration between Peter Szolovits, Jon Doyle, and William J. Long at LCS, Isaac Kohane at Children's Hospital, and Steve Pauker at New England Medical Center. The goal of Guardian Angel is to design and build a distributed system that collects medical data, monitors the progress of medical conditions, educates the individual, and constantly monitors the patient as a kind of "sanity check." The system is built with palm-top computers, desktop machines, and servers—all connected with a variety of networking technologies. One of the early applications that the group is exploring involves tracking the blood sugar levels of insulin-dependent children. The levels will be automatically recorded using a specially modified blood-glucose meter and then transmitted through the network. The system will monitor long-term trends and sudden spikes; if the sugar levels are dangerously low or high, an alarm might be sent out through a wireless network.

Medical information becomes even more valuable in the context of the information marketplace. Just imagine: People could instruct their personal computers to take the information collected by the Guardian Angel system to seek out clinical trials from which they might benefit.

They might take their medical data and submit them over the Internet, in a safe and secure manner, to a clinical diagnosis system, which would return predictions of their future health and possibly recommended diet changes. For people considering risky medical procedures, the information marketplace would enable them to learn how other people with similar medical conditions fared after the procedure and rate one set of hospitals and practitioners against another.

Turning such visions of the information marketplace from predictions into realities requires more than top-notch computer science research. It takes dedicated individuals and organizations who see their mission as an evangelical one and who will make the concerted efforts required to move inventions from the laboratory into the world at large.

Notes

1. Michael Dertouzos, "The Information Marketplace," in *Electronic Mail and Message Systems: Proceedings of the American Federation of Information Processing Societies (AFIPS) Workshop on Technical and Policy Perspectives*, Washington, D.C., December 1980.

2. Gail Jennes, "In His Own Words: An MIT Expert Foresees Computers That Clean, Mow Lawns, and Become Playmates," *People* (August 30, 1976): 26–28.

3. W. Diffie and M. Hellman, "New Directions in Cryptography," *IEEE Transactions on Information Theory*, IT-22, no. 6 (1976): 644–654.

4. Although MIT did not believe this at the time, this information appears to have been at least partially true. In December 1997, British Intelligence's Communications–Electronics Security Group (CESG) released a paper by retired CESG officer James Ellis—"The Story of Non-Secret Encryption"—describing the invention of the RSA as well as the Diffie–Hellman algorithms by members of CESG in 1973 and 1974 (available at http://jya.com/ellisdoc.htm). As far as the algorithm's security goes, even twenty-two years after the discovery of the RSA encryption algorithm, the fundamental mathematics appear to be sound, and the algorithm itself has not been cracked.

5. Michael Dertouzos, *What Will Be: How the New World of Information Will Change Our Lives* (New York: HarperCollins, 1997), 84.

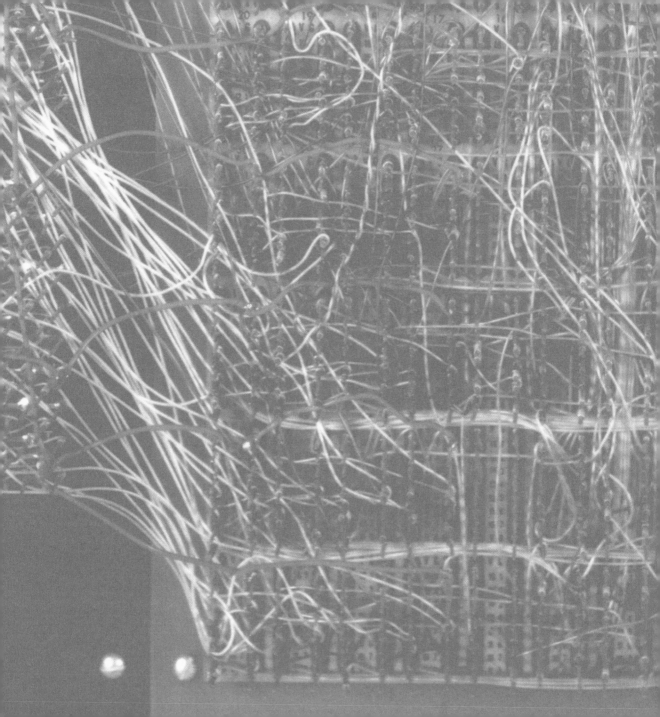

The Next Thirty-Five Years

Thirty-five years after the founding of Project MAC, it is difficult not to be impressed by what has been achieved. The information utilities envisioned by Fano, Corbató, and McCarthy are so pervasive that they seem mundane. A hundred million people share in Licklider's Intergalactic Network, exchanging data at speeds up to a billion bits per second, via the data connections designed by Clark, Reed, and Metcalfe. The Information Marketplace, exemplified by Berners-Lee's World Wide Web, is the technological phenomenon of the decade. Spending over the Web shall soon surpass a trillion dollars annually, with each penny spent secured using the algorithm dreamed up by Rivest in the spring of 1977.

The ARPA Information Processing Technologies Office (now DARPA/ITO) is once again directed by an LCS alumnus with a vision for networking. Where Licklider promoted information communities, David Tennenhouse has a different message for today's computer science researchers: "Let's Get Physical. Let's Get Real. Let's Get Out. Let's Get Active." That is, researchers need to make more of the physical world accessible to computers through sensors and actuators, create real-time systems with dramatically lower latency than is available today, get users out of the loop, and leverage mobile code to make this all happen.

Just as Project MAC invented interactive time-shared computing to support an information community in Technology Square, LCS and the AI

Lab are today planning an active network architecture for MIT's new Computer Science building. Called Oxygen, the system will feature "intelligent rooms" with vision and speech interfaces linked to handheld computers in a self-organizing network. "The basic idea behind Oxygen . . . is about being able to do more by doing less," says Michael Dertouzos. By using using small computers that are "close to the user," the two laboratories, working together once again, will become an incubator and showcase for a seamless, ubiquitous information infrastructure. Designed to support both mobile computing and seamless collaboration, Oxygen may become a prototype of the systems that will replace desktop computers in the coming years.

But great research laboratories must also look beyond the next several years, and beyond popular expectations. In the early 1960s, time-sharing was an outlandish, even controversial, notion, and Licklider's program at IPTO was criticized as a waste of government funds. "The main reason why people objected to time-sharing was that computers were very, very expensive, and cycles should not be wasted. Many felt that one should look carefully at the results of a computation before proceeding to do more computations. Saving people's time and effort was not a popular idea," says Fano. He remembers speaking with a famous scientist of the day "who felt that it was improper, almost immoral, to allow somebody to be on-line with a computer."

And what of today's outlandish ideas?

- On the 4th floor of Building NE43, Richard Stallman and a small group of programmers are coordinating the efforts of thousands of volunteers around the world. Together they are building a new operating system complete with application programs, a graphical desktop environment, and programmer's tools. Together they are creating a new operating system—one that is similar to the UNIX operating system, but with one important difference. Unlike UNIX, which is the creation of Bell Labs and is now sold by many companies, the GNU operating system is *free software.*

"The word 'free' doesn't refer to price," says Stallman. "It refers to freedom." Although people do give away Stallman's software—he says that copyright protection of programs is a betrayal of society for personal gain—the true distinguishing feature of free software is that people are free to modify it to do what they wish. Stallman started Project GNU in 1983; his goal was to create a global community of computer programmers and users who could exist outside the world of closed, proprietary software.

Since then, Project GNU and the Free Software Foundation, a nonprofit charity that Stallman created to write programs, have been tremendously successful. Although GNU has yet to ship its own operating system, Stallman's tools have formed the bulk of four others: NetBSD, FreeBSD, OpenBSD, and Linux. The success of these systems, and the global movement that Stallman helped to create, is just starting to have a serious impact on the world of business, finance, and commerce.

- On the 9th floor of the building at Technology Square, at the very spot where the Interface Message Processor (IMP) once connected Project MAC to the nascent ARPAnet, sits something new for the building: a biology laboratory. The lab is run by Tom Knight, who helped install that same IMP thirty years ago.

    "The dominant science for the past fifty years of computing has been physics and semiconductor technology," says Knight. "The technological foundations of computing for the coming decades lie in biology and organic chemistry." In the new lab, Knight is coaxing bacteria to be the workhorses for a technology of "cellular computing," where circuits operate within living cells using digital-logic signals represented as concentrations of DNA-binding proteins rather than as electrical voltages. "We want a cell where we can say turn on this gene, turn off that gene," he says. In a similar vein, Dave Gifford is shuttling between his office at LCS and the Biology Department, where he has been encoding state-machines as sequences of DNA. Their experiments hint at a world of "amorphous" information systems composed of a myriad of biological cells, where programs control the action of pharmaceuticals or the precision fabrication of structures at microscopic scales.

If such visions seem radical, we should ask: Are they as radical today as interactive time-sharing was in 1960? Thirty-five years from now, at the seventieth anniversary of Project MAC, will they seem equally mundane?

Name Index

Abramson, Norm, 27
Adleman, Len, 48–50, 51–52
Allen, Larry, 36
Asente, Paul, 35
Atkins, Derek, 52

Berners-Lee, Tim, 54–59, 65
Boyack, Steve, 47
Bressler, Bob, 25
Burner, Wes, 32

Cain, Thomas, 54
Cerf, Vint, 28, 32
Clark, David, 21, 22–25, 28–32, 37, 65
Corbató, Fernando J., 3, 5, 6, 7, 8, 9, 12, 17, 32, 65
Crocker, Steve, 27
Cuseur, Gerry, 59

Daggett, Marjorie, 4
Daley, Bob, 4
Dennis, Jack, 4
Dertouzos, Michael, 12, 32, 33, 41, 44–47, 50, 56, 58, 66
Diffie, Whitfield, 48
Doyle, Jon, 61

Fano, Bob, 6–9, 12, 17, 65, 66
Fredkin, Ed, 4, 12, 59

Gardner, Martin, 49
Gettys, Jim, 35–36
Gifford, David, 53–54, 56, 68
Glaser, Ted, 10
Goldwasser, Shafi, 52
Gorry, Anthony, 59, 60
Graham, Bob, 10
Gray, Paul, 33, 51
Gumpertz, Rick, 24–25

Hellman, Martin, 48
Holloway, Jack, 28

Inman, Bobby, 50

Kaashoek, Frans, 16–17
Knight, Tom, 28, 44, 67–68
Kohane, Isaac, 61

Lerman, Steve, 34
Licklider, J. C. R., 4, 5, 6, 12, 24, 37, 44, 46, 59, 65, 66
Liskov, Barbara, 35
Long, William J., 61

Martin, Bill, 59–60
McCarthy, John, 2, 4, 6, 7, 65
Metakides, George, 56
Metcalfe, Bob, 25–27, 65
Micali, Silvio, 52
Miller, Steve, 37
Mills, Dick, 9
Minsky, Marvin, 6–7, 12
Moses, Joel, 12, 32–33, 59

Needham, Roger, 36–37
Neuman, Clifford, 37
Neumann, Peter, 11

Pauker, Steve, 59, 61

Reed, David, 28, 65
Reid, Brian, 35
Ritchie, Dennis, 10–11
Rivest, Ron, 47–53, 65
Roberts, Larry, 24
Russel, Steve, 4

Saltzer, Jerry, 5, 8, 11, 12, 22–23, 26,
    32–33, 34, 35, 36, 37
Scheifler, Bob, 35–36
Schell, Roger, 11
Schiller, Jeff, 37, 52
Schroeder, Mike, 10, 24, 36–37
Schwartz, Bill, 59
Shamir, Adi, 48–50, 51–52
Sherman, Alan, 54
Siegel, Arnold, 4
Stallman, Richard, 36, 66–67
Stratton, Jay, 6
Sussman, Gerald, 59
Szolovits, Peter, 59–61

Taylor, Bob, 24
Teager, Herb, 4
Tennenhouse, David, 65
Thompson, Ken, 10–11

Vezza, Al, 25, 56–57

Ward, Steve, 14–15
Weizenbaum, Joseph, 9, 59
Wilson, Gerald, 32–33, 34

Zue, Victor, 42–44